EYE OPENERS
Trains

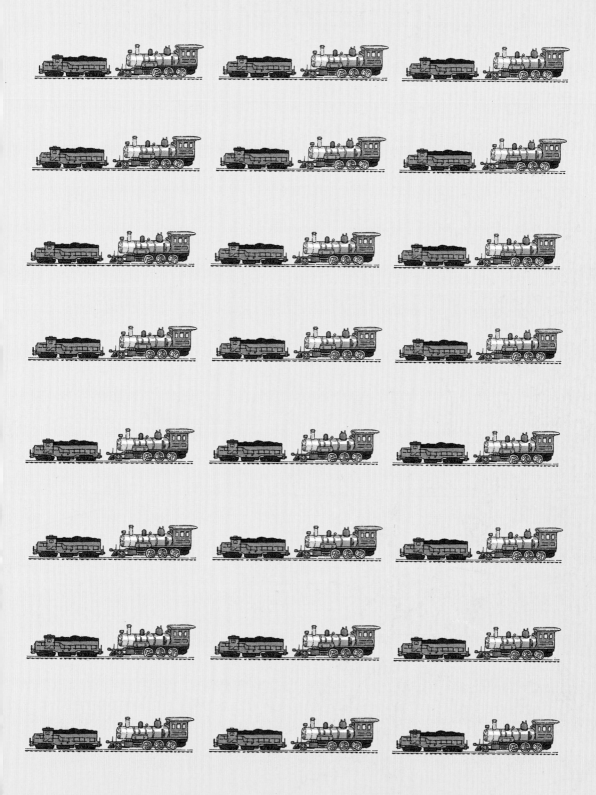

www.dk.com

Editor Stella Love
Designer Mandy Earey
Managing Art Editor Chris Legee
Managing Editor Jane Yorke
Production Jayne Wood

Photography by Dave King
Additional photography Tim Ridley
(pages 4-5 and 8-9)
Illustrations by Jane Cradock-Watson
and Dave Hopkins
Modelmaker Ted Taylor
(pages 10-11, 14-15, and 16-17)
Train consultant Julian Holland
Train models supplied by Victor's, London,
and Beatties of London

Eye Openers ®
First published in Great Britain in 1992
by Dorling Kindersley Limited,
9 Henrietta Street, London WC2E 8PS

Copyright © 1992 Dorling Kindersley Limited, London
First paperback edition, 1999

A CIP catalogue record for this book is
available from the British Library.

ISBN 0-7513-5953-X

Reproduced by Colourscan, Singapore
Printed in China

EYE OPENERS

Trains

Written by Angela Royston

DK

London • New York • Sydney • Delhi

Steam engine

This steam engine is very old. The fireman puts coal on the fire to heat a boiler of water. Steam from the hot water makes the engine go. A loud whistle tells people that the train is coming.

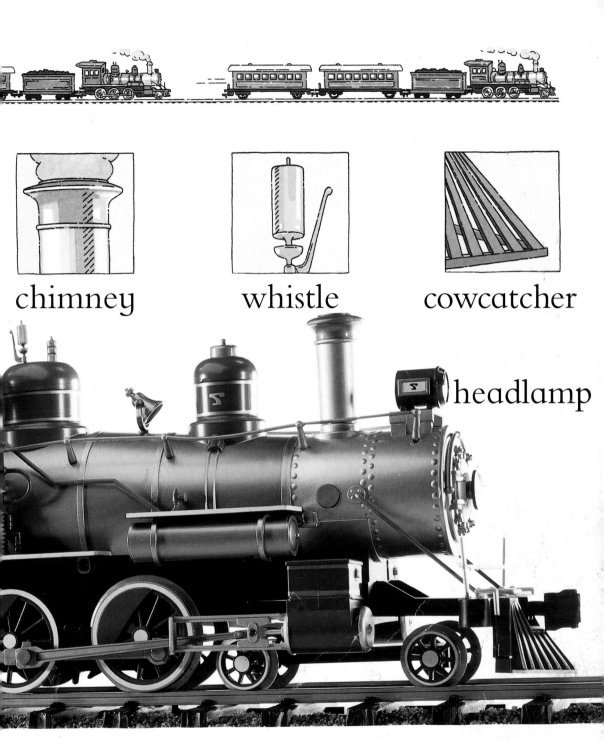

chimney

whistle

cowcatcher

headlamp

High-speed train

This train travels very fast.
The engine uses electricity
from a wire above the track
to make it go. The train
tilts as it speeds round bends.
This makes the ride very
smooth for the passengers.
They can hardly feel that
the train is moving.

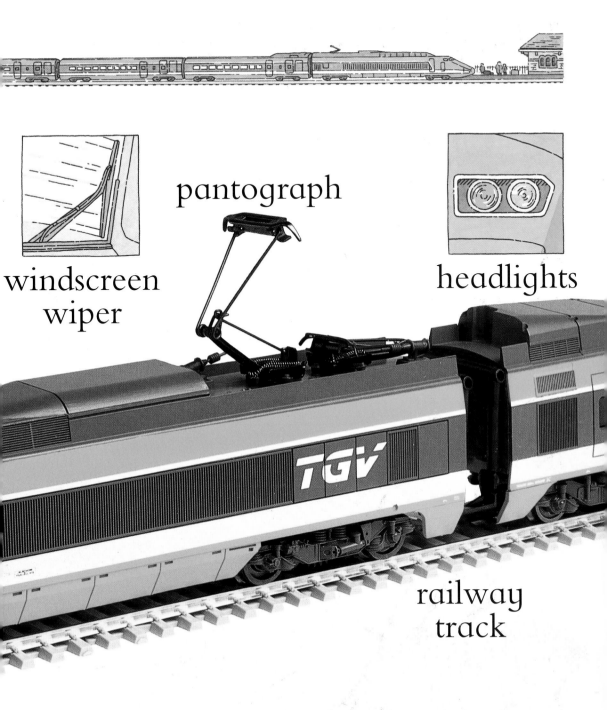

pantograph

windscreen
wiper

headlights

TGV

railway
track

Breakdown train

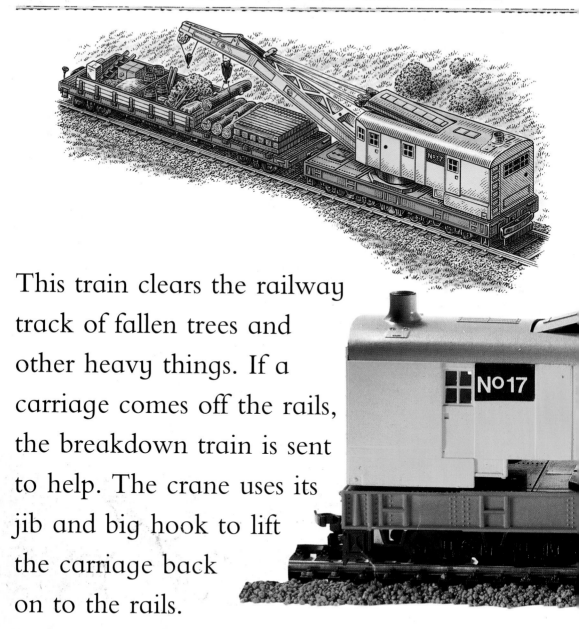

This train clears the railway track of fallen trees and other heavy things. If a carriage comes off the rails, the breakdown train is sent to help. The crane uses its jib and big hook to lift the carriage back on to the rails.

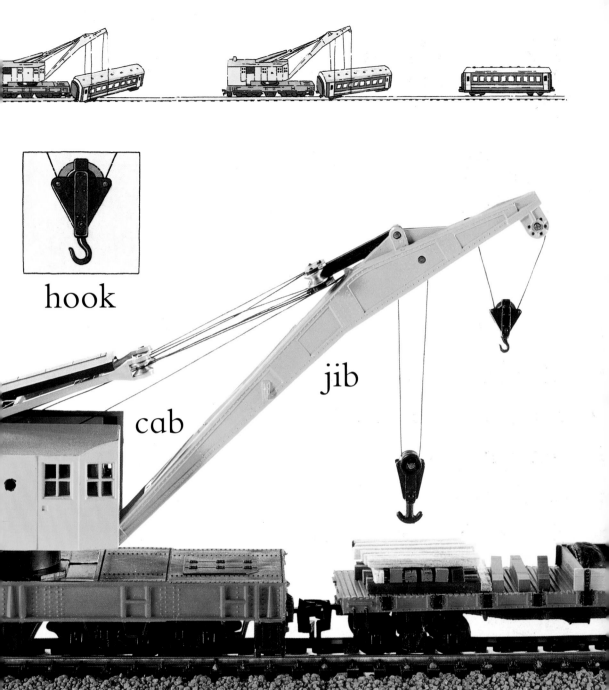

hook

jib

cab

Crocodile train

The crocodile train
pulls carriages high
up into the mountains.
The long engine bends at
each end. This helps the train to
go round the steep mountain sides.

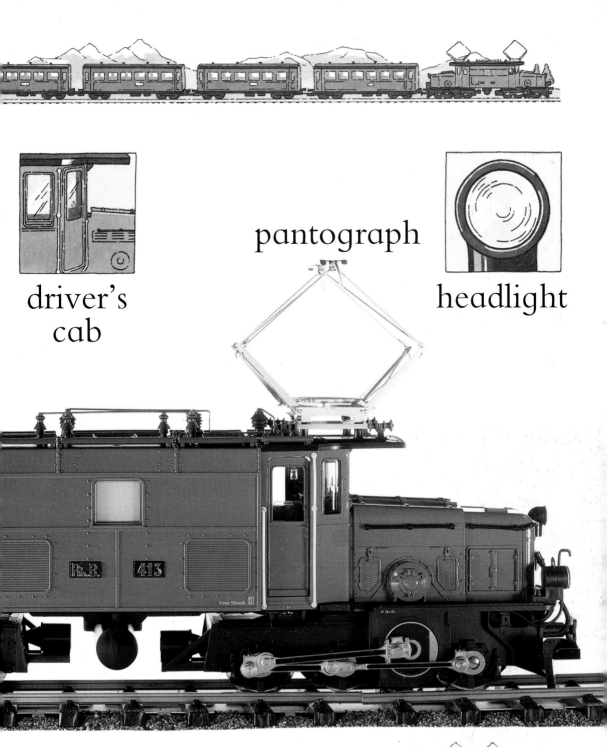

driver's
cab

pantograph

headlight

13

Passenger train

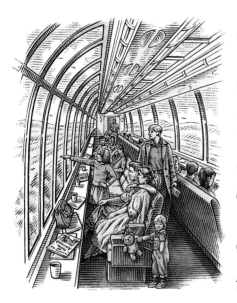

This big engine uses diesel oil to make it go. It pulls double-decker carriages on long journeys. The passengers can sit back and enjoy the view as the train speeds along.

carriage

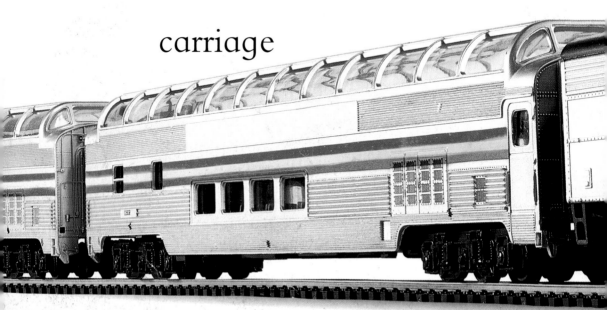

horn

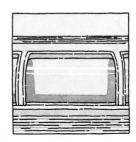

window

cab

Goods train

A goods train transports all kinds of heavy loads. The tank wagon carries oil. Some box wagons are cooled to keep food fresh on long journeys. The last wagon is called the brake van.

brake van   wheel   ladder

tank
wagon

box wagon

Shunter

The shunter is a strong
engine that works in the
railway yard. It pulls goods
wagons across the yard to the
unloading site. The shunter
also pushes carriages into the
train sheds at the end of the day.

engine

06 005

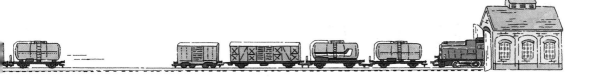

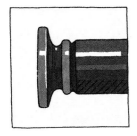
buffer

wheels

window

carriage

Orient Express

The Orient Express is a famous old train. It carries people on short holiday trips. Passengers like to travel in the old-style carriages. Meals are served in the dining car. At night, the passengers sleep in bunk beds in the sleeping car.

air vent

door

window

sleeping
car

dining car